PIVOT POWER

25 Ways to Zig Zag Your Business Successfully Through This Crisis. And the Next One.

STU LLOYD

HOTHEADS INNOVATION LTD

Cover design by: Stu Lloyd

CONTENTS

Title Page   1

Copyright   2

Foreword   5

My Introduction to Pivoting   10

It's Now or Never.   16

Er, Excuse Me, What's a Pivot?   19

So what does a Pivot look like?   22

 Aggregated Take-outs   56

The 'Pivot Power' Toolbox   58

Ready. Fire. Aim.   64

The 'PiVOT POWER' Pivot business consulting   67

Acknowledgement   69

About The Author   71

Praise For Author   73

Books By This Author   77

FOREWORD

Growing up in southern Africa was an absolute adventure wonderland for me. Being free to play on the sugar cane farm – which extended as far as the eye could see -- was great for stoking our imaginations, making us greater risk-takers, and building our self-confidence. Because there was opportunity and crisis lurking everywhere ... be it a deadly poisonous *mamba* snake curled under a rock in our garden, be it a bee-hive in a tree that we felt we should smoke out (tip: don't do this), or be it galloping on horseback at full-stretch across recently ploughed fields.

Weekends were the best, because that's when we went down to the Dudley Pringle Dam, nearby. Early morning, the water would be like a mill-pond – flat and glass-like. Perfect conditions for waterskiing, so we'd launch the boat – called *Imvubu* meaning hippopotamus in Zulu -- and a few hours of thrills and spills would ensue.

When I say spills, oh, I'd wish we'd had a video camera back then to capture some of the spectacular wipe-outs my brothers and I had. Except, perhaps, for the time my older brother Glendon had a wild fall in which the ski slammed down on his head so hard the keel split his head open. Lucky it was a fresh-water dam otherwise the blood would've attracted sharks from miles around.

As I said: opportunity and crisis everywhere.

By mid-morning usually the wind would come up, so the choppy water was no longer good for skiing. So we'd put the speedboat away, and we'd launch *Daisy*. *Daisy* was our first-ever yacht, a little Optimist-class dinghy, which is perfect for learners because it's very forgiving and allows you to make massive tactical errors, but very rarely tip you over into the water.

And so Dad set about teaching us sailing. Although the rigging on an Optimist is supremely rudimentary – you have one rope and a rudder – you soon learn about harnessing and harvesting the wind. There's a whole new lexicon to learn, too, words such as running, reaching, hauling, heading up, etc. These all referred to the all-important angle of the sail to the wind.

In other words, similar to the strategic direction in your business.

I saw this for myself when another sailor in the same type of boat was going roughly in the same direction as I was, but perhaps at a 5-degrees different angle, and he would pull ahead with a churning wake, leaving me scratching my head and wondering why I'd ever taken up this dumb sport.

Then there were a whole bunch of other terms such as jibing, tacking, going about. These are all ways of turning the boat.

In other words, similar to the tactics available in your business.

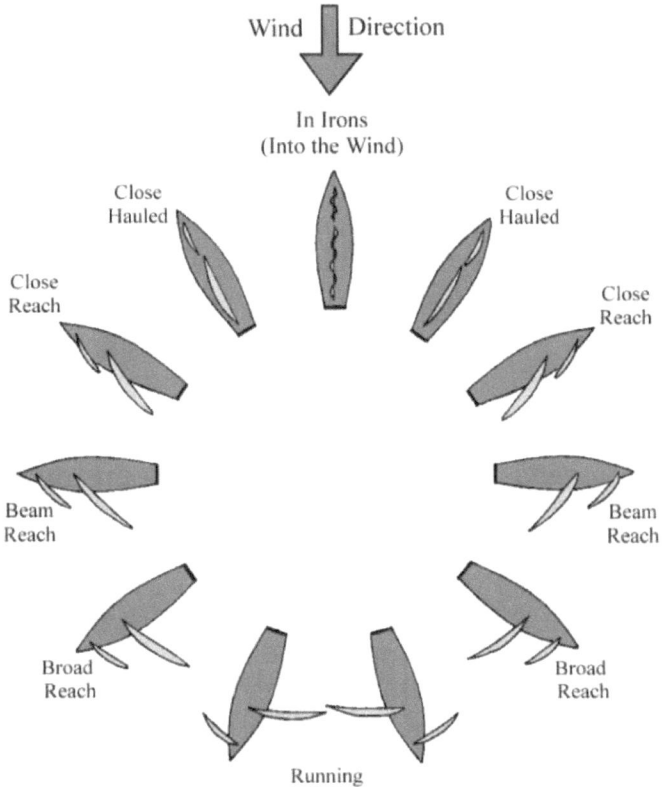

(Source: Princeton University Sailing Club)

One mind-blowing fact I learned is that yachts can actually sail faster than the wind. This is usually between a beam reach (90° to the true wind and a broad reach (about 135° away from the true wind). This involves a lot of trigonometry obviously, so I was more a gut-feel sailor.

Which would probably explain why the term I got most frequently acquainted with was "getting in the irons." This term dates back to the days of the big old wooden sailing boats transporting prisoners shackled to the deck in irons.

Getting in the irons refers to when you sail directly into the wind. Often it might be the most direct route to your target, but it cannot be done. It's literally a no-go zone. Your sail flaps wildly, hither and thither, searching for the wind, which just rushes right past it because there's no angle of resistance. Worse still, it's really difficult to steer out of it in order to find the wind because you have no momentum. So you find yourself drifting backwards, further than ever from your objective.

And in a race day – and in business -- nothing gives your competitors smugger pleasure. Which is how *Daisy* and her crew came to be not-so-proud winners of the wooden spoon prize, which was usually a bailing bucket or something similar, on a regular weekly basis.

The only thing worse than getting in the irons was "turning turtle". This means your yacht is completely upside down with the mast pointing vertically downward in the water. This is not good.

With the essentials of sailing under our water-logged belts, we upgraded to a twin-hulled Hobie Cat. Wow! That was an adrenaline-inducing ride. The principles remained the same – only the stakes were higher. Get your sail angle right and you were literally flying along on one hull, feeling it lift under you, higher, and higher, and ... slam! You suddenly found yourself airborne and tangled in ropes and sails and you were underwater.

You discovered the very fine and fickle line between peak performance and total disaster.

The latest generation of America's Cup yacht race contestants sum this up perfectly. They're able to sail as close as 20° to the wind. Most impressively some are able travel at *twice* the speed of the wind. One New Zealand boat was recorded belting along at nearly 48 knots (88km/h) in just 22 knots of wind.

Take a moment to Google some race footage now. Exhilarating adrenaline-inducing stuff to see them tearing along in one direction then suddenly scything away in another to cross the finish-line nano-seconds ahead of their competitors. Get it wrong though and crew-members have been known to die.

And that is exactly what this book is about:

How to change direction in business when the trade winds that used to be favourable are not blowing for you anymore. How do you rig yourself up to find the next productive burst, and get you closer to the finish line, faster, with your crew (and all its limbs) intact. And -- most of all – how do you get yourself out of the irons in a full-on crisis, and hopefully even turn it into an opportunity?

I'm pleased to say, we actually became reasonably good sailors, and the bailing bucket prizes started going to someone else. When we immigrated to Australia, we upgraded to an even bigger Hobie Cat. And got to the stage where my father, as skipper, would have all his three teenaged sons in harnesses on tip-toe, leaning out possibly 3 metres above the churning surf, to keep the boat balanced and upright.

Later, in business as an intrapreneur and entrepreneur, that experience gave me an invaluable feeling for when we needed to tack, sail closer to the wind, or run for home.

Because of that success, nowadays, fortunately, most of the sailing I do is aboard a friend's large seagoing yacht at sunset on Sydney Harbour, with a beer or wine in hand.

So, welcome aboard -- I wish you plenty of smooth sailing ahead.

Stu Lloyd
Locked down in Sydney
April 2020

MY INTRODUCTION TO PIVOTING

Back in 2003 I was packing to fly from Sydney to Hong Kong as part of a book promotion tour. There were distant grumblings coming out of southern China and Hong Kong about some kind of weird new unknown virus.

In the words of The Clash song: "*Shall I stay or shall I go*?" I called a long-trusted doctor in Hong Kong, Peter, and asked him. "As long as you wear a mask on the plane home you should be fine," he said, somewhat nonchalantly.

On arrival in Hong Kong I was shocked – all the immigration officials wore masks and there was a hovering air of menace. In the bustling streets, everyone wore masks. I reached my hotel and flicked on CNN. Guangdong and Hong Kong were headline news. The epicenter of SARS, as they called this new virus. And the severity continued to build and build and build over the ensuing five days I was in the city.

Finally I made my flight home, mask squarely in place on my face. Half way to Australia, an older Chinese lady collapsed in the aisle next to me and a call went out for any doctor on board. We felt under siege in this tin tube at 35,000 feet. She was carted off when we landed in Brisbane, the plane then to continue on to Sydney.

I re-boarded the plane – possibly the only passenger from Hong

Kong carrying on through to Sydney, and definitely the only one wearing a facemask. The domestic Aussie travellers, jaunting from Brisbane to Sydney looked askance at me, like I was some kind of weirdo wacko. (Full disclosure: they may have a point!). But what struck me is that they had no idea this plane had just flown in from the SARS epicenter. That a passenger had taken ill on this very plane. And now here they were breathing in that same fragrant Hong Kong air and touching those remote controls and seat belt latches.

By the time I reached Sydney, SARS was a full-blown pandemic. Over 8000 became infected, less than 1000 of those died. But it was enough to knock the stuffing out of the Asian markets.

Sales of my books, which were happily riding high on best-seller charts in airports across Asia, fell off a cliff overnight. They never recovered. The fat cheques which used to find their way under my door each month all but dried up. I had one son at an expensive private school, and a daughter about to start.

And so I was introduced to a new word in my vocabulary: pivot.

What is in my existing armoury, my skill set, my capability, my competence, that I can leverage and re-purpose and turn into dollars -- fast?

Well, I can write. So I applied to the Australian Society of Travel Writers for membership; they rejected me. I meantime found a few friendly editors to publish some of my ramblings, banked a few small cheques, then reapplied successfully.

Soon I was flying, sailing, and riding all over the world on hosted media trips and selling stories to inflight magazines, major daily newspapers around the world, and – my crowning glory – a 3,500 word feature for *National Geographic Traveler* on the Trans-Mongolian train trip, from Moscow, across Russia, through Mongolia, ending up in Beijing.

Here I met Qing Yan, an anesthetic doctor who was the daughter of a very eminent surgeon in China. They had both essentially treated Patient Zero in the SARS outbreak, being locked-in with their patients at the hospital for 3 weeks. She told me of the fear, the uncertainty of dealing with that deadly unknown.

But soon, the halcyon days of being a latter-day Hemingway seemed to be closing in. Newspapers – under pressure from digital disruption and this new-fangled thing called the internet -- were merging and rationalizing their businesses. Where once you had one travel editor per publication, they were all set adrift, and one group editor replaced them. Where once you could sell the same story to those eight different editors, now you could only sell your story once. They took digital rights to your story as well, and – if you were lucky – threw in a couple of extra peanuts as payment for that.

Demand imploded. It was time to leverage and repurpose my skills again – fast!

So I accepted the challenge of a huge national tour operator to create, curate and lead special interest military history tours through Southeast Asia. One of my passions is World War Two in the Japanese theatre, and they'd read some of my war story articles. Soon I was taking the relatives of veterans through Singapore, Malaysia and Thailand: "So, your Uncle Fred was probably behind that tree there with his machine-gun glowing red hot ..." I told one traveller, "David, the reason you didn't sleep well last night was because this is the exact hospital camp site where your father was interned, the worst camp on the whole Death Railway."

To tell those stories and bring closure to those people was the most rewarding and fulfilling work I've ever done. Yet weirdly, it was nothing I'd ever set out to do – it just turned out that way because of successive pivoting.

Then came the Global Financial Crisis. I got cleaned out unceremoniously, a massive part of the small fortune I made from selling out my ad agency to a US-listed multinational group vaporized before my eyes. All passive income now ceased.

It was time to leverage and repurpose my skills again – fast! (Can you sense a theme building here?)

So I started accepting again the calls for consulting that were coming in. Facilitating pow-wows from companies that found themselves in suddenly dire predicaments. How do we zig-zag our way through this? How do we build the agility and creativity of our teams?

My background degree was psychology, and I'd always maintained a passion for it. But now it was becoming sexy because the MRI scanner was opening up exciting new avenues of enquiry. I dived deeply into that, and designed and delivered science-based programs to build creativity competencies in corporates.

I studied additional certifications in the fascinating field of neuroscience and neuro-marketing. And added business storytelling to my roster of talks and programs because – *duh!* – I'd been a professional storyteller for nearly thirty years (if you include my formative years as an ad agency copywriter and creative director).

I am only qualified to talk about two things based on my experience: creativity and storytelling. Fortunately these have both been identified as must-have 'future skills' by just about every institute on the planet.

So I have been spending about 200 days on the road, consulting, speaking, and training Fortune 500s around Asia Pacific. Sometimes I pinch myself – like when I come off stage from unleashing on a ballroom full of 1000 executives. I'm buzzed, they're buzzed. In the words of David Byrne from Talking Heads: "*And you may ask yourself, well how did I get here?*"

But unlike travel writing, I don't get to stop and explore the places I'm in – just an endless rodeo of airports, hotels and function rooms.

Fortunately it's lucrative work. So now at the end of each year I take a 'writing sabbatical' for a few months in which I stay home, research a topic, write a book about it, create a training program around it. And then the circus starts up again.

But January 2020 was different. Because the circus didn't start up again. There were grumblings coming out of China … you know how that story goes now.

Suddenly clients were sliding work out to July and beyond. "Any availability in September?" Six months of workshops and keynotes were cancelled or postponed overnight.

It was time to leverage and repurpose my skills again – fast!

So it is that I find myself replacing face-to-face work with alternatives. Scurrying to upload online video training programs that I'd filmed and edited, but never marketed. Scurrying to transfer a two-day live business storytelling skills event into a two-day Zoom session. Scurrying to cobble a collection of funny Asia-related travel stories into a book to offer some escapist fun to people in lockdown. (It worked well – it took me just two weeks to produce and hit the #1 spot in two of Amazon's category charts within four days of launching!).

And now I'm scurrying to get this book out – giving myself just one week to do so -- and offer a pivoting skills program online because I think this is what companies need most from me at this moment.

And because I want to embody the theories I preach.

What's interesting is that I already had the outline plan for this program completed five years ago, according to the file date in my computer. I just never went hard with the execution and marketing, until now.

Why not? Well, I think that's the thing with business. Things are often a luxury until they become a necessity.

Pivoting skills are now a necessity. For you, and for me.

Not just for the current crisis, but for the *next* one which will come around in similar viral form from the same source, a global cyber-hacking meltdown because of all the back doors left slightly ajar by the race to work remotely, and the *next next next* one -- the post anti-biotic world full-on Armageddon Apocalypso.

They may or may not happen in that order, but that's another story. Regardless, don't panic -- pivot.

IT'S NOW OR NEVER.

'When?' is often one of the consideration factors in implementing any plan. Is it today, next week, this quarter, this financial year?

But procrastination is a management tool in itself. Especially when it comes to innovation. It's easier to say 'no' and the whole thing goes away. Or just let it slide, so it's not technically a 'no' but neither did you raise your head above the parapet either.

Speaking with my son, Justin, the other day, he relayed what was happening with his workplace. He is involved in manpower planning for a large healthcare provider. So they are super busy at this time as you can imagine. They're often acknowledged as a leading employer, with a renowned focus on work-life balance etc. But a groundswell of voices requesting for more work at home time -- as recently as February 2020 -- was solidly rebuffed: "Impossible ... technically impossible ... impossible ... just impossible ... no."

Here he is now just one month later working happily, successfully and productively from his lounge room.

So how did the impossible become possible?

Covid-19 put a gun to our heads. 'When' has been taken off the table for us. Vietnamese-Australian comedian Anh Do is keen on relating his father's advice: "There's only two times – there's now, and there's too late."

Square co-founder Jim McKelvey, writing recently in *Entrepreneur*, agrees: "Now is often the right answer."

Covid has arguably done more for fast-tracking digital disruption than your CEO, CIO, and CTO together have done in the past decade. It's achieved it in weeks.

Much of this change is related to underlying trends which had been simmering for a while, only now with the blowtorch turned high on them.

The time to act is now. We need to do something, *anything*, because your ship is headed for the rocks.

Which reminds me of advice given by my karate *sensei*: "If someone jumps you, do something, *anything*, even scream like a crazy girl if you have to, because it'll startle your attacker and buy you time to think of your next structured move."

In other words, some response is better than no response. Even if it's a slightly 'wrong' response, it at least sets the process for change in motion. That's the thing: we can fine-tune it later as we go along.

There's never one right answer. If we're lucky there are several good answers, and we choose one. But waiting for the 100% perfect wave will only have us dashed on the rocks.

Now's the time to ditch the 100-page business plan, too. You don't have time. By the time it's perfected and polished, the market's moved on. I've always argued that there was never time for a 100-page plan and I'm pleased to find some heavyweights in my corner on this.

Step forward please, Linda Rottenberg. Her research for the book *Crazy is a Compliment* turned up the following fascinating findings on Inc 500 companies:

> ➤ **Only 12% conducted formal market research before they launched.**

> ➤ **Only 40% wrote formal business plans (and, of those, two-thirds ditched them later!)**

"But, but, *but* ...!!!" I hear the MBA readers gasping. I shall go on ...

"Business plans rank no higher than 2 (out of 10) as a predictor of a new venture's success," says Bill Sahlman, entrepreneurial finance guru at Harvard Business School. "Smart businesses adapt and change."

Still not convinced? Don't make me do it – here's what another guru has to say on it.

"Guessing the right strategy at the outset isn't nearly as important to success as conserving enough resources," said Clay Christensen, "so that new business initiatives get a second or third stab at getting it right."

I love the fact he used words like "guessing" and "stab". It speaks of something far more visceral than most managers would allow. Hint: as much as you'd like it to be, it's not all science. And it's not all certain.

Even one of the greatest statistical minds of the 20th century, George EP Box, cautions us: "All models are wrong, but some models are useful."

So where does that leave us?

We've learned so far that we need to have an action bias. Do something *now*. Today. Before lunch. Hopefully it's something that people will look back at in three years and say: "Remember during the Covid Crisis, Jane did that amazing thing. And thanks to her, wow, look at our company rocking now!"

We're going to work on that amazing thing. It will come to you by the end of this book.

ER, EXCUSE ME, WHAT'S A PIVOT?

Two buzzwords have arisen from this crisis so far. One is Zoom and the other is Pivot. Both are nouns, but their real power is as *verbs*.

"We'll *Zoom* at 3pm Tuesday, Ok?" You know your brand has made it when it becomes a verb. (I wish I'd bought shares in Zoom four months ago.) We *Google* answers. We *Hoover* the floor. Hey, is that just coincidence -- all those examples have a 'double O' in them?

And every start-up and company and corporation has been thrashing the word 'pivot' in the last few months.

The word 'pivot' itself is not that exciting: "The central point, pin, or shaft on which a mechanism turns or oscillates," according to the *Oxford Dictionary*.

Even *The Lean Start-Up* author Eric Ries' definition doesn't exactly incite a riot: "A structured course correction designed to test a new fundamental hypothesis about the product, strategy, and engine of growth."

I prefer to paint pictures of jet skis zig-zagging across the bay, switching back and forth, turning on a dime. Or imagine those America's Cup yachts.

The secret is the angle of the sail to the wind. And that's our challenge in business – to find the perfect positioning, product offering, service, solution, price, that's going to keep the sails full for maximum speed and return on effort and investment.

The problem is that many of our businesses – ironically the bigger, most successful businesses – act more like a super-tanker than a jet-ski. Set on a strategic course across the ocean, and barely able to adjust for the rocky atolls, pirate attacks, and stealthy enemy submarines along the way.

To continue the analogy further, the conundrum is the keel.

The keel size reflects the size of your boat, the history of your company, and relative top-heaviness of your load. Meaning the bigger your vessel, probably the deeper the keel you need for stability. But a keel also produces drag and friction. It weighs you down. And it's a full-time job to scrape off the accumulated barnacles growing on it. That's your bureaucracy.

Meanwhile, start-ups and SMEs, are spinning and pirouetting around you in their jet skis. More agile, nimble, flexible. Darting this way and that.

What's the point of all that showboating?

To find a better tack to fill our sails and find the future faster.

A pivot is not change for change's sake. It's a change towards something more profitable, more rewarding, more purposeful, more achievable, more sustainable. Some of the best analytical thinkers in business – Bezos, Gates, Fred Smith, Dell – are fond of making *continual* strategic improvements: Cheaper, faster, better.

Usually, deciding whether to pivot or not is something a founder or CEO will lose a lot of sleep over. Do we leave this harbour that we know and head into the rough and choppy waters beyond? Which brings us back to the whole procrastination thing.

Because it's a leap of faith hopefully over (and not into) the Mariana Trench, the Valley of Death. It's the "Struggling Moment" as Bob Moesta once called it in the *Harvard Business Review*.

Discovery planning is a way of checking that our thinking and our underlying assumptions are still robust. What do we know? What don't we know? What's the greatest strategic uncertainty? In many ways we're experimenting and checking to prove that our thinking is *wrong*. If it's not, great, then carry on. Otherwise, fine-tune, zig-zag and pivot towards that new true north.

"A pivot requires that we keep one foot rooted in what we've learned so far, while making a fundamental change in strategy in order to seek even greater validated learning," says Eric Ries.

Much of his celebrated pivoting riff is about testing a "new fundamental hypothesis" about the product, business model, or growth engine.

But in times of crisis it looks more like this: "What the hell can we do to keep the doors open and the lights on?"

And, as you'll see shortly, out of this can come great insights, inspiring creativity and boundless possibility.

It's amazing what we can think of when we have a gun at our head.

SO WHAT DOES A PIVOT LOOK LIKE?

Name any famous company, and chances are that what we see now is not what they started out as. And we might even discover moments when they just about went under and disappeared from sight altogether, before the skipper reset the sails and – WHOOM! – caught that sail full of wind that set them on the sea to stardom.

Most pivot examples in the textbooks are product related, and we'll get to those later. Products (especially tech products) always seem to be shinier and get all the media play.

But pivots come in all shapes, sizes and flavours, and – apart from Product -- can be applied to Process, Premises, Promotion, People and Purpose (the 6Ps of Innovation as I group them). All of these areas can be innovated by a pivot.

Bear in mind, each of these 20 pivots is named for the dominant strategic characteristic of the play. But the lines between them can be blurry at times and some pivots can fuse a few techniques simultaneously.

Process Pivot

In business we take an element of bureaucracy for granted, and there's often a positive correlation between the size of a company and the slowness of the system. It's the keel I mentioned earlier, and it causes Corporate Drag and Corporate Lag.

Now, as punkishly impetuous as I am, I get that as long as a process is a process, it needs to be followed. But it doesn't mean that the process itself can't be innovated. Tweaked for effectiveness and efficiency in the interest and service of speed as a competitive weapon.

And if a small trial of the new process works in one business unit, then it can be rolled out across the enterprise.

Netflix
When Netflix started its exponential growth curve, its team size grew, and its back-room systems grew accordingly. A few years ago, a quick analysis of hiring admin people to track things like petty cash, taxi voucher claims, etc was going to run an annual salary bill of around $2 million dollars. Instead, Patty McCord, chief talent officer, didn't hire more people, she pivoted the process – got rid of the need for signatures and approvals – and introduced a company expense policy.

Just five words long, it read: "Act in Netflix's best interests."

People knew exactly what was expected of them, and if found in breach, they'd be in serious trouble. In the meantime front-liners could get on with their mission-critical work, less encumbered by expensive, time-consuming, mind-numbing paperwork.

Premises Pivot

How we use retail estate – for our own back-room teams as well as customer-facing functions – can be challenged or constrained by changes in demographics or buyer economics.

Let's see once this Covid Crisis washes over and some sort of normality resumes. My gut feel is that there will be a New Normal made up of a much greater percentage of people working from home permanently, with less physical office attendance. This means less need for prime office space and commercial buildings. This will force landlords in turn to search for their own pivots to maintain revenues via alternative creative space usages.

Ikea

While their 25,000 square foot blue-and-yellow megastores have become ubiquitous in major cities around the world, Ikea has been toying with smaller stores for the past 5 years because their modern customers prefer to shop online from home (also possibly because car ownership rates are falling). A few clicks and they're done. The new stores are 40% smaller, include just a few room setups, and of course no meatball restaurant. A digital VR component enables customers to select products which are then mapped virtually to their room to take the guess work out of it.

Unilever

In Singapore there's been a fascinating Premises Pivot in play with the launch of LEVEL3, a co-working space that pushes the boundaries of collaboration, co-working, and corporate innovation. LEVEL3 brings together Unilever staff, startups, and entrepreneurs onto one floor of Unilever's offices. All Unilever employees are able to descend an internal staircase to mingle with others, most of whom are there to be a part of the Unilever ecosystem, and enjoy a casual coffee together.

Another interesting Premises Pivot was made by WPP, Unilever's communications agency, who have moved their 50-person Team Unilever to sit and work permanently in Level 3 for closer cohesion and speed with their client, calling it "the marketing services ecosystem of the future." Ironically this is almost a Retro Pivot (see below), given that in 1899 the Lintas agency was formed as an in-house agency for, yes, Lever Brothers, the forerunner of Unilever.

Promotion Pivot

Uppermost in our minds as intrapreneurs and entrepreneurs needs to be the consideration of how new customers will discover your new product, service or solution. What Eric Ries calls the 'growth hypothesis.'

One of the biggest pivots in the past decade has been away from mass media ad spend, towards online digital spend. It's been a very jagged course because new media, new platforms, new channels, new measurement tools have all surfaced, and we've had to learn in real time as we went along.

Brands that just stuck steadfastly to analog media are probably missing out a lot in audience engagement and dialogue.

P&G
P&G and Google did a people swap (there's another People Pivot opportunity for you to try), embedding teams in each other's organisations for 3 months. P&G were launching a new baby-care product, and sent out the usual invitations to media to attend the press launch. The Googlers looked down the list of attendees and said, "Hey, where's your influencers?" Say what? A quick conversation then ensued about motherhood and baby-care influencers who had followings in the millions – far more reach and resonance than some of the invited magazines. The influencers duly turned up, and garnered tons of love for the new products. P&G learned a lesson and have always had influencers on invite lists ever since.

The tone of messaging too has had to change as the younger generations coming through are less in thrall of 'hypodermic' top-down one-way communications (which mass market brands enjoyed for half a century). Frankly Millennials are too darn cynical of anything that smells remotely like an ad. But they can still be engaged, just in a far more human tone, and more engaging manner. Talking *with* them rather than to or at them.

Here, I like to talk about my 5-step 'VOICE' System. Brands need to pivot their messaging towards being more Vulnerable, Original (authentic), In the Moment, Congruent and Engaging. Because resonance beats reach every time.

Emily Veg Sticks

One great pivot as a result of Covid was by Emily Veg Sticks snacks in the UK. They'd already booked their outdoor poster campaign, so it had to run. But at the last minute they chose to be 'in the moment' and acknowledge that, with everyone in lockdown, very few would actually see their messages. So this is what they came up with instead:

**'Hmmm ... maybe we should have made
a TV ad instead.'**

'Our first poster ever. Seen by a runner and one pigeon. Typical.'

**'Do an ad when it's warmer, they said. More
people will see it, they said. Fffft.'**

Uber

Uber, too, changed their TV ad message to end with; "Thanks for NOT riding with us at this time." Nice in the time of social distancing.

Transferwise

As a startup with the mission to save people fees on sending money around the world, they felt marketing should be easy. So they went to Google and spent up on search terms that indicated clear and strong intent to transfer money internationally. It was only marginally successful – mainly because most people didn't realise they were being ripped off by bank and incumbent services.

So they pivoted towards customers as advocates instead. "Getting our customers to trust us was hard, getting our customers to trust their friends was easier," said Neilan Peiris, TransferWise's VP of Growth. It was a more scalable channel without the expense and trust issues that plagued their paid marketing efforts, and resulted in profitable referral loops and a Net Promoter Score around 86%. As the #1 transfer provider in the world now, their team has grown from 40 just eight years ago to over 1750 now.

People Pivot

We can pivot who and how we hire, and how we retain people. Already in the 'gig' economy, greater numbers of people are working on a contract basis rather than as full-time permanent employees. And the Inclusiveness and Diversity movement is speeding ahead, causing a sharp pivot in who is now considered (or not) for positions.

GM
General Motors put its culture of inclusion in to practice by partnering with outside groups, such as the Michigan Alliance on Autism.

Slack
Partnered with The Last Mile, a program to train and up-skill former prison inmates in technology. Three graduates already joined Slack.

Travel Daily
This Thailand-headquartered global travel news group is renowned for their high-spirited Thirsty Thursday monthly industry gatherings in major cities around the world. With their clients now in lockdown, the slight pivot here is "internal" Thirsty Thursdays, according to founder, Gary Marshall. "We get the staff together, and we use it to keep in contact with *our* people, and to learn more about them, what pets they have at home, etc."

Purpose Pivot

As we feel an increasing need to find our 'why' and Millennials exert pressure on employees to stand for more than a single bottom line, 'Purpose' is becoming the new 'Free Massages at Work'. Start-ups are hard-wiring purpose into who they are and what they stand for from Day One. Think Tom's Shoes and their buy-one-give-one model. More established companies are having to pivot towards it.

The danger here is the possibility of 'greenwashing' and becoming inauthentic. What you say must equal what you do, otherwise you *will* be called out, and named-and- shamed on social media and possibly even mainstream media.

All businesses that thrive in the future will look a lot more like the social entrepreneurships of today, with a meaningful purpose at their core. It's part of what I call 'Soul Quotient' or SQ.

Unilever

Unilever are moving in this direction with "sustainable living brands." Their research shows that 2/3 of consumers around the world say they choose brands because of their stand on social issues; and over 90% of Millennials say they would switch brands for one that champions a cause.

Millennials are already the biggest segment of employees in the USA and will constitute 35% of the global workforce by next year. Nine out of 10 Millennials live in emerging markets so Asia will be very heavily impacted.

Their spending power will surpass that of Gen X in 2020, and continue to rise and rise. This will make them the most powerful segment both as consumers and as employees.

This means that they will shape businesses from the outside and from the inside, based on the desirability of their product/service offering, and their desirability as workplaces.

In 2018, Unilever's Sustainable Living Brands – 28 of them – grew 69% faster than the rest of their business. "We believe the evidence is clear and compelling that brands with purpose grow," said Alan Jope, CEO. "Purpose creates relevance for a brand, it drives talkability, builds penetration and reduces price elasticity. In fact, we believe this so strongly that we are prepared to commit that in the future, every Unilever brand will be a brand with purpose."

Dogfish Head distillery

This Delaware distillery stepped up when it seemed supply of sanitizer was dangerously low during the Covid Crisis. They knew for years that they had the ingredients and wherewithal to make it, but just never pursued it. It sells its sanitizer to the State government at what founder Sam Calagione calls a "fair market rate." But this is where the Purpose part kicks in. 100% of the proceeds from the sanitizer sales will be donated to a newly created relief fund called the 'Restaurant Industry Emergency Action Trust' that provides financial aid to local restaurant industry workers who have been laid off as a result of the crisis. Calagione and his wife admirably contributed $50,000 to establish the fund.

Zoom In Pivot

One of Eric Ries' pivot types for lean start-ups, in this situation one feature of an original product or solution becomes the whole product. Let's look at Instagram to understand this, and also to understand that Instagram – like so many of the world's highest profile brands – did not come into this world fully formed in a singular blinding flash of inspiration. Far from it.

Instagram

Burbn was a check-in app that included gaming elements from Mafia Wars, and a photo-sharing element as well. Burbn provided a very average user experience, too cluttered for many, and it crashed and burned. In looking at the data among the ashes, Kevin Systrom and Mike Krieger noted that the photo-sharing part of the app was popular and well used. So they iterated a version of the app that zoomed in, literally, just on photography. And Instagram was born.

Toys 'R Us

In similar fashion, a department store crumbled. But the owners noted that there was one profitable department: toys. So they culled everything else, and reopened with just toys and a new name, Toys 'R Us. Sadly they ran out of creative gas and hit the skids a few years ago. A renaissance is in process, so let's see what pivot they use to rebuild this time.

Zoom Out Pivot

This is the opposite of Zoom In, where sometimes new features, departments, services and solutions might be required to make a sustainable and attractive offering. The poster child here would be Amazon.

Amazon

It started as an online bookstore. And interesting to note that no bricks-and-mortar bookstore giants like Borders were able to pivot to a formidable digital presence.

As it built up, so the Zoom Out pivot began, and it became the one-stop one-click 'everything' store. Which sort of goes against marketing wisdom of owning a niche in your consumer's mind. But they nailed the experience. (We'll talk more about Amazon under Platform Pivot below.)

YouTube

YouTube wasn't always YouTube. Did you know it started life as a video-based *dating* service? It's classy slogan was 'Tune in, hook up.' That's right. Users could upload short videos of themself describing their ideal partner, and also browse the site for potential matches.

The data and feedback hinted at the potential of becoming a broader host of online videos. So YouTube pivoted into cute kittens and epic fails and slowly turned itself into a sexy $65 billion empire that Google wanted to hook up with.

Customer Segment Pivot

Peter Drucker was fond of asking: "What does the *customer* value?" A 'Job to Do' in Design Thinking speak is identifying a customer's problem, which is a great – though not foolproof– way to start finding solutions that rock their world. Eric Reis calls it the 'value hypothesis', checking whether your solution really does deliver value to users.

Often times, early testing and results you get with early adopters can be misleading because, by definition, early adopters have different mindsets and behavioural patterns to others. Success with this group does not necessarily translate nor scale to mass market.

So a Customer Segment Pivot is one where you get most of the answer right in that you *do* solve a problem … but not for the person you initially had in mind. Often this can be because people use, or see a use, for your product that you didn't see.

Vertex
Vertex was a B2B manufacturer of wipes for cleaning industrial machines, electronics, and so on. Somehow a policeman got access to these, and found them deeply satisfying for deep-cleaning his hands after dealing with the "scum" out on the streets of his average shift. So he wrote a letter to the factory, pleading for their wipes to be made in more customer-friendly packages and sizes.

The factory gained an insight and responded with suitably amended products and packaging, becoming a highly successful B2C mass market player in the process.

North American Aerodynamics
This company was founded in 1964 and became a world leader in accuracy parachutes, most of which have military and adventure sport applications. Come the Covid Crisis they realised they could solve a problem for a different market segment – by making Level 1 masks for frontline health workers using their manufacturing experience with specialty fabrics.

Play-Doh
In the post-depression 1930s, a white squidgy spongy product, made by Kutol, was used as a wall cleaner to clean the black residue on walls left by coal heaters. However by the 1950s, as oil and

gas heaters took hold and vinyl wallpapers appeared, Kutol found demand for its product falling off a cliff. Scrambling for direction, the owners learned from one of their sisters-in-law, a teacher, that she had been using the cheap product in arts and crafts class to make ornaments. The kids loved it. Knowing the business was in trouble she urged them to shift focus to this stuff as a toy. They simply removed the detergent from the dough, added almond scenting, and some cool colours. Oh, and changed the name. Then went off and marketed it to kindergartens. To date more than 2 billion cans of Play-Doh have been sold worldwide.

Jeremy Cowart

Jeremy is an award-winning photographer whose mission is to explore the intersection between creativity and empathy. Usually he's photographing Kardashians, Taylor Swift, Ryan Seacrest, Keith Urban, and ... you get the idea. Then came the Covid Crisis. So with A-listers on the sidelines, he hatched the idea of #seperatetogether in which he photographs people who are physically separated by lockdown, then joins them in an image.

"I got to photograph a daughter in Bali, Indonesia, alongside her Dad in Syracuse, NY. I got to photograph a brother/sister duo ... she was in Boston and he was in Japan. One of the most special moments was photographing Gayle, who has yet to meet her grandbaby in person. We even got the baby to look to her left and smile!"

In just the first two weeks Jeremy, who was named Most Influential Photographer on the Internet by *Huffington Post*, photographed individuals, families, healthcare workers, and now loved ones separated by Covid in a remarkable 750 photo shoots across 48 states and 25 countries.

"I can't believe this idea is working," Jeremy says. "If you would have told me a month ago that I'd be doing this, I never would have believed you. But here's to pivoting, right?"

Customer Need Pivot

Sometimes we identify that our target customer has a problem worth solving. We believe it to be a red-hot opportunity. (Such as a book on pivoting during a crisis, for example!) But sometimes the problem is not exactly the same one we anticipated.

And sometimes the customer doesn't value that problem as highly as we think they should. So we're talking to the right people, and we can do something valuable for them if we just tweak our current offering a bit to suit. This tweaking can sometimes just be reframing or repositioning in their mind. Sometimes there needs to be physical or material changes to the product or solution.

A classic Customer Need Pivot example is the tobacco industry. Sales continue to grow on a global basis, but have clearly slowed in Western markets and show growth in emerging markets. Overall the major tobacco suppliers realise that the increased regulation and taxation of their product means they are in a sunset industry situation. So with medical cannabis seeming to be a megatrend it's no wonder that tobacco companies are buying up cannabis farms and greenhouse capability in a huge way.

Starbucks

These ubiquitous coffee shops did not start out as the magical 'third place' they are today. Back in 1971 they were selling espresso makers and coffee beans. Schultz came to work for them later, and, after his visit to Italy in 1983, was convinced that European-style coffeehouses could be all the rage in America. His boss (the owner) didn't agree. But he did agree to back Howard's venture on condition that he buy Starbucks' coffee beans.

The first cafe was an exact replica of the Italian coffeehouses – with no chairs, standing room only, and opera music. Early adopters fed back saying: close but no cigar. So he introduced chairs, turned off the opera music, and made it more comfortable and spacious so people would linger longer. It was the magic experience people wanted, and Shultz ended up buying out his boss's coffee bean factory and rebranding the whole lot as Starbucks.

(As an aside, Starbucks was almost called Pequod's. Would it have been as sticky? Who knows. But name changes often appear in pivot stories of companies: Micky Mouse was originally called Mortimer, but Walt's wife felt it was a mouthful. Disneylandia became Disneyland at the last minute. Kutol's Rainbow Modeling Compound became Play-Doh. And so it goes. And we haven't even talked about rock megastars yet. So do not underestimate the power of a killer name.)

Wrigley's

William Wrigley Jr moved to Chicago and started work as a soap and baking powder salesman back in the 1890s. He had the idea of offering free chewing gum with each purchase, and the gum proved to be more popular than his core products. Wrigley went on to manufacture his signature Juicy Fruit, Doublemint, and Spearmint flavours. He brand was sold to Mars for over $20 billion dollars a decade ago.

Avon

Ding dong! Avon is synonymous with makeup, cosmetics even fashion. But it started, similar to Wrigley's, when David McConnell -- a traveling book salesman -- realized that his female customers were more interested in the free samples than his core products. Those samples were perfume that came with the books. So he began recruiting sales ladies for his perfumes, believing correctly that they'd connect and convince better than their male sales counterparts.

Pinterest

Tote allowed people to browse and shop their favourite retailers and sent updates when their favourite items were available or on sale. But studying the usage data, the founders realized that their users were more interested in curating and building 'collections' of their favourite items, and sharing these collections with friends. So it pivoted to reflect that preference, and repositioned itself as Pinterest. It skews heavily female with 80% of its users being women. While the user-base has grown astronomically, they are still trying to move towards Tote's ecommerce roots, so watch out for a Value Capture Pivot sometime.

Twitter

Twitter began life as a network called Odeo, where users could find and subscribe to podcasts. When iTunes moved into the podcast niche, the founders Jack Dorsey and Biz Stone felt it was time for a pivot. A hackathon was called for, with employees given two weeks to come up with new ideas. The idea of a status-updating micro-blogging platform was conceived and implemented.

Pepsico

As half the world heads inexorably towards an obesity crisis, and sugar becomes the new tobacco, consumer goods companies like Pepsico face an existential crisis. Under the design thinking-driven leadership of recently departed CEO Indra Nooyi and guidance of Mauro Porcini, they are pulling off a classic Customer Need pivot. Their brands are now divided into two camps – 'Good for you' and 'Fun for you'. The latter houses all their high-sugar cash-cows which still pump billions into the machine to allow them the time and resources to find their equivalents in the healthier options section. This is an ideal situation for companies to leverage without walking away from their core business overnight.

Levi's

During the 1850's Californian gold rush, a young entrepreneur headed out west with the idea of selling tents to the thousands and thousands of miners. But he discovered there was little demand for tents because of California's mild climate. So next came a bold Customer Need Pivot. He cut up the strong cotton material of his tents and retailored it into hard-wearing trousers that he sold to the miners instead. The entrepreneur's name was Levi

Strauss, so you probably know how the rest of that story worked out.

Buildadesk

The Clarke Murphy Print company has been in the Murphy family in Sydney for 5 generations. They print stuff. Except in a Covid Crisis people stop needing stuff being printed. So in an inspirational moment owner Benn Murphy pivoted to serve families like his – which includes 4 daughters – suddenly working from home. "Our dinner table became a work desk and home schooling area. I wanted a way to separate the two," he says. If he was having this problem, others might be too.

Literally overnight buildadesk came into being – self assembled cardboard tables strong enough to hold up to 80kgs. A bonus was the assembly itself became a fun kids activity, and one model even features colouring-in panels to keep the kids busy. A website was cobbled together within two days, and they were in a new business, although leveraging the existing in-house industrial design and packing/dispatching capabilities of their print business.

Isoking

Jeremy Fleming and his team at Stage Kings are usually feverishly busy with building staging and structures for major events like Commonwealth Games, Ninja Warriors, and super-group rock concerts and festivals. Suddenly everything on their 2020 order book was cancelled. A friend recommended they turn their hand to isolation furniture, especially as they had a CNC router – a computer-controlled cutter. The Isoking range was born – 16 wooden products including standing desks, monitor stands, wine racks (well, alcohol sales are up significantly!) and perspex retail counter guards. The flat-pack desks take "30 seconds" to assemble.

"Our 'why' has changed for now," says Jeremy. "Three and a half weeks ago we thought it would be a good idea to start making work-from-home office furniture to try and keep our lights on, and keep some of our crew busy. Now with our team and a bunch of other amazingly talented event people, we're making 150 desks a day, keeping 52 staff busy. Mindblowing!"

Competitor Pivot

We can change our company (Business Architecture pivot), our customers (Segment Pivot) and we can also change our competitors. Some fertile ideas can arise by pivoting away from your current competitors and aiming to compete with another set entirely. Why? Perhaps we want to move into a higher yield area, or perhaps our current playground is a red-ocean sharkfest.

Lexus

Toyota built a reputation for solid and reliable cars, frankly seen as cheap and no-frills by many. As good as a Ford, let's say. But the sexy and profitable end of the market is the luxury car market in the US, Europe, and increasingly Asia. The competition there was mainly BMW, Mercedes and Audi. There's no way to sell a $100,000 – or more – Toyota to the status-conscious upper classes. It just wouldn't deliver the badge value.

So in aiming to compete against BMW and Mercedes instead of Ford and Volkswagen, a serious pivot was needed in style, technology, performance, and marketing. The result was Lexus – completely devoid of connection and association with Toyota in every way possible. And they now stand a respectable fourth in the global luxury car sales rankings.

Coopetition Pivot

Is your competitor always your enemy? No. Often we align in industry bodies and marketing alliances. Rising tide floats all boats, and so on. How could you co-operate with your competitor/s instead of against them?

Samsung/Sony

Samsung Electronics and Sony formed an agreement to share research and development costs in designing and developing flat screen LED televisions.

EDX

Harvard University and MIT formed EDX, a non-profit that provides free online courses, each initially investing $US30 million. It's now grown to 140 institutions offering over 2500 courses.

Ventilator Challenge UK

The Covid Crisis gave rise to a fantastic example of collaboration and co-operation in the form of the Ventilator Challenge UK (VCUK).

VCUK is a consortium of 14 firms including Airbus and Rolls-Royce, BAE Systems, Ford, McLaren, GKN, Meggitt, Renishaw, Thales, Siemens and Ultra Electronics. They have all come together to develop and produce ventilators for the UK government, which is critically short.

Dyson snared an order for 10,000 of its CoVent model, designed in just 10 days. But as it was designed from scratch (leveraging Dyson's knowledge of suction and ventilation) it needs to pass specification testing by the NHS.

VCUK's plans – Project Oyster and Project Penguin – leverage two existing designs with the idea of rushing out up to 30,000 ventilators produced in parallel by harnessing the combined manufacturing muscle of the consortium. Apart from lending factory floor space and logistical know-how, the companies have redeployed some of their most skilled engineers from key company projects to work on the ventilator effort.

Business Architecture Pivot

Author and organisational theorist Dr Geoffrey Moore contended that companies generally follow one of two business architectures: a high margin-low volume (complex systems) model, or low margin-high volume mass market (volume operations) model. The two are mutually exclusive – you cannot be both at the same time – with complex systems typically being more common in the B2B arena. But note that pivots involving switching between the two are certainly possible and often desirable.

Nokia

Remember the days when a Nokia smartphone was *the* phone to own? Nokia may be in desperate need of another pivot now, but that doesn't detract from the successful pivoting it did to reach this stage already. Nokia started life as a Finnish paper mill in 1865 – a big manufacturer with a B2B architecture in place. Throughout the 20th century, they explored new markets, creating a wide variety of products such as rubber goods, electronics, cabling, and then telecommunications devices such as a car phone. In 1992 they entered the red-hot mobile phone sector, a B2C play. Their success in the same year prompted them to focus exclusively on mobile devices, selling off all other divisions. So it was also a Zoom In pivot, right? Turnover increased five-fold over five years in the mid-90s.

Pixar

Pixar essentially started in 1974 as the Computer Graphics Lab, under the New York Institute of Technology. Within five years, George Lucas had enticed them across to form the Graphics Group, then part of the Computer Division of Lucasfilm. But they were developing hardware and software, and creating just small amounts of actual film outside of product demos. All the while they held the sacred dream of creating the world's first computer-animated movie. The company was spun off and acquired by Steve Jobs in 1986, freeing up long-serving founders John Lasseter and Ed Catmull to create the powerhouse creative studio we know it as today.

Value Capture Pivot

"Can we make money doing this?" One of the most important questions to ask when evaluating a potential new avenue (see Toolbox section for more). The next question is *how* do we make money from this, and this is at the heart of the Value Capture

Pivot. The way you charge clients and customers has implications for all aspects of your business – especially in terms of product/solution development, and marketing strategies.

The internet has democratized a lot of things, but worse, made a lot of 'free' stuff available, such that it anchors many people to believe that nearly all content should be free somehow. You need to justify your value and your existence daily.

Word of warning here: "Free" is a great marketing come-on and it suits the budget of a lot of people – but that model is not sustainable. So we need to explore and answer how we monetise this, and turn this into commerce or ecommerce for profit.

Psyblog
One of the favourite blogs I follow, Psyblog, delivered daily doses of psychology findings and research free to my inbox each day. Then one day I noticed a change. There'd be a juicy topic to read about but only if you were now a 'member'. Premium blog content was marked with an 'M' (for members-only) next to it. You had to pay a subscription to get access to that higher-level good stuff. It then becomes a value proposition judgment call: do I value it at $x per month? I'm sure they lost a lot of faithful readers, but at least they're getting paid for the work they're doing now, and not just building goodwill in a community for no return.

Subscription models have become a go-to of the New Economy. Netflix is a great example, but it didn't pivot to that, it started with subscriptions baked-in to their model.

Adobe
Adobe on the other hand offered individual products that you bought, from a shop, on a CD-ROM. You then went home, or to your office, installed the CD and installed the program from there.

It was Salesforce that really disrupted the software market, making everything downloadable from the internet. And now you couldn't imagine doing it any other way. But in terms of value capture, Adobe pivoted from a price-point-per-product model to a subscription model, under which there's an array of software and services available to you under your plan. For example on their Creative Cloud for around $50 per month you get access to all 20+ of their creative apps, which would individually cost you $300+ per month. The marketing point here is that's attractive because they're bundled, you can access all (which you may or may not use) but the incremental cost to Adobe is $0. Their share price has risen 440% in 5 years.

Of course, Value Capture is always enhanced by the 'instant upgrade' enticements. For just an extra $10 a month, you can enjoy all of this too. Click. Money in the bank. Wix websites are good at this. You can build a cool website for free. But if you don't want their little logo in the corner, you need to upgrade to make it go away. If you want to send emails to your database, that's a pay-for plug in, and so on.

Carlton United Breweries

In the Covid Crisis, although alcohol sales look like being generally up, *draft* beer has been a big casualty. Usually drunk fresh at pubs, within days of manufacture from the tap, there are now over 100,000 kegs around the world sitting waiting to be poured down the drain. (I know.) The Australian government cut a deal with the brewers to refund the taxes and allow the pubs to sell them in bottles to customers for take away consumption.

"We're donating 20,000 resealable bottles to more than 100 pubs in Melbourne, Sydney and Perth," Carlton United Breweries CEO, Peter Filipovic, said. "It'll also give many people their first taste of tap beer from the comfort of their own home." Patrons are enjoying the experience so much, they're even calling for Zoom hook-ups so they can drink 'with' the workers in the pub, and some hope this can continue as a New Normal.

Some hotels are pivoting by doing attractive "pay now, stay later" deals. This captures the cash flow now – albeit at steeply discounted rates (some examples I've heard are around 50% off) – and the guests will come enjoy their stay when the time is right. It ensures the hotel stays around.

Amazon

Having become the 'everything shop' platform (see next section), Amazon soon learned they could make significant cash out of ads for that retail, too. Plus, charge a premium for featuring retailers in more visible positions. In 2019 Amazon's ad business grew by 40% to over $14 billion. Plus, of course, a percentage share of their sales.

Anonymous photographer

A photographer from Australia confided in me his very clever Value Capture Pivot, so I'm leaving him un-named here. Typically, commercial photographers work on a half-day rate, or a full-day rate, and negotiate with clients accordingly. He felt, for his efforts, he was leaving a lot of money on the table.

So he pivoted. His new pay scale was this: "Ok, you want two photographs of your factory, that'll be $1000." Didn't matter the time involved, it was outcome-based. But once he was on location, he'd cover off the two required shots, then shoot as much of everything else around the place that he could. The clients would 'Ooh' and 'Aah' over these extra shots, and suddenly they'd want to buy 8 or 10 images. So his order value went from $1,000 to $10,000 just like that. *Kerching!*

Platform Pivot

The best way to think of a platform is something that other things can sit on top of. Like Microsoft. They essentially have a platform monopoly on PCs. Because of that, all developers make sure that whatever software application they are designing and developing is compatible with sitting on top of a Microsoft operating system. (I wrote that explanation as much for *my* benefit as much as yours.)

Many founders have vivid daydreams of their solution being the master-mega platform for future products and apps to sit astride – Bill Gates has certainly inspired generations – but the main obstacle is developing your own single killer app first. Another obstacle is that most customers are looking for a single solution, not a whole platform.

Amazon

We've talked about how Jeff Bezos pulled off his Zoom-Out pivot. But another masterstroke was the thing that could have killed him and his business: opening up Amazon as a platform for all resellers of every damn thing under the sun. The chorus of "No, Jeff, don't do it, Jeff!" rang out from every sane business analyst in the world. Because, on the surface, it looked like he was inviting the cannibals into his own kitchen. But it worked because Amazon became the one-stop 'everything' store destination we now know it as. Everyone depends on being on his platform. And, instead of killing him, it made him the richest man on the planet.

ebay

eBay made its first big splash as a platform for auctioning collectables and other stuff (full disclosure: as a stamp collector I bought a ton of collectables there, and as a musician I sold a lot of musical gear there). But eBay has pivoted too -- shifted its focus to becoming a leading e-marketplace, a classified ad service, as well as an online ticket vendor through acquisition. Its big difference to Amazon is that it does zero warehousing and fulfillment itself.

Growth Engine Pivot

Who doesn't want faster growth and more profitable growth? Most bosses would be happy with that. But a Growth Engine Pivot is hooking your business (whether start-up or established) to some sort of growth-hacking technique. That's how Facebook, Uber, Tinder, etc, got so big so fast.

It could be something organically viral or a paid growth strategy. The beauty is that scaling digitally costs the business zero in terms of marginal cost of replication. An extra customer for Spotify or iTunes or Airbnb costs them nothing extra.

Airbnb

What really put start-up Airbnb on the map was the masterstroke of hooking up with Craigslist, which had a database of millions of users. They offered their host listings the chance to link with one click (via some sneaky coding) on Craigslist as well. So suddenly they were all over Craiglist, and people became aware of this thing called 'Air Bed & Breakfast.' All their listings 'popped' too because Airbnb insisted on higher quality photography and better copywriting, which they offered as a free value-added service. Their hosts were excited because their average earnings went up by $500 per month.

Another growth engine hack was to offer all Airbnb members $25 when their friends travelled. So, of course, the members were getting members for them like crazy. "Hey guys, there's this new thing, and if you stay somewhere for a weekend, you get a great experience and I get $25. Let's do it." Wildfire! Groupon built its empire the same way – if we all do this, we all win, so let's do it. So, deals and offers were spread virally by the members themselves.

And therein lies the magic of New Economy marketing: help your customers do your marketing for you.

Hotmail

Millennials would never believe you when you say there was a time when email didn't exist. And when it first started it was clunky and expensive, with long strings of numbers instead of your name. And then came Hotmail.

It started small but used its users to hack its growth. As a free service it leveraged its right to add these sentences to each email signature: "This email sent with Hotmail, Join Hotmail now" and "Get your free email at Hotmail."

Possibly the most successful viral growth hack ever. The cost? Zero! Customers did their marketing for them.

IBM

IBM embodies several pivots, dating back to 1911 when 3 manufacturing companies merged to become Computing Tabulating Recording (CTR). Only when Thomas Watson took over in 1924 did it become International Business Machines (IBM) and build its reputation as Big Blue, the super-computing giant. Then came the PC boom, which they dominated (platform domination example – you *had* to be 'IBM compatible') but then IBM got slowly strangled as the rest of the world worked out how to make cheaper me-too models.

In a desperate moment, IBM then chose to make one of the boldest moves by pivoting away from its core business towards providing IT consulting services for large organisations.

"We can no longer separate out the product from the experience we build around it," is how Nancy Hensley, former Chief Digital Officer, explained it. "That's a big shift for us in a large organization." While they could never go back to "thinking like a startup" they had to embrace growth mindset.

"It has truly shifted from an outbound approach to growing the practice to an inbound one," says Jason Barbato, growth strategist at IBM. "Product teams and other service areas now come to growth hacking with their analyses and ideas in search of our expertise." Today, IBM is in good shape, worth more than US$150 billion and is home to Watson, the AI platform that slayed human chess champions, competitors on the TV show Jeopardy, and is at the centre of many a Fortune 500's AI efforts.

Lego

"The brick is at the heart of what we do, but we are using digital to enhance it," is how CEO Niels Christiansen sees his empire's pivot. Lego is back from the brink of extinction around the turn of the millennium, when they were perceived as an old school legacy toy out-shone by the new screen games. But then a burst of creative love was thrown at the brand. Now there are 10 Legoland theme parks around the world, *Lego Movie 1* and *2*, and even a primetime 'reality' TV show, *Lego Masters*, in which teams compete to create outrageous designs. In the corporate world, Lego Serious Play has been introduced as a problem-solving tool. These days, to make it a more hybrid experience, digital planning tools are available for kids to pre-plan and visualise their constructions. And all of these things have served to sell more coloured plastic bricks, with Lego posting profits of over \$500,000,000 last year.

Channel Pivot

In a Channel Pivot you essentially produce the same product, service, or solution, but you are finding more efficient and effective ways to get it to your customers, whether it's B2B or B2C.

Examples of this abound in the New Economy because direct digital sales and distribution channels have mushroomed. Look no further than books as an example. Before, if I had an idea for a book, I'd have to do up a nice pitch proposal, hand that over to my agent, he'd then have lunch with a number of publishers, who'd then decide whether they shared the enthusiasm for said idea, at which point the book went into production (involving editors, typesetters, art directors, and printers), was trucked across the land into book shops, and waited for book readers to find it on the shelf. A lengthy process in itself, then even lengthier as the author sweated on sales reports and royalty checks.

Using this book as an example: I had the idea on Saturday 18 April, started writing it on Monday morning, and it was for sale online at Amazon by Monday 27 April.

Channel Pivots usually involve an adjustment of sorts to do with pricing (an e-book or e-album is way cheaper than their physical counterparts). Maybe they offer a different feature. For example a recent travel-related book I launched offered a 45-page sample chapter to cross-sell another of my travelogues (an unaffordable consideration in a print book). There might also be competitive positioning adjustments, as you'll often notice with any company with the word 'Direct' in their name. Insurance companies come to mind.

This often implies a relatively frictionless online experience, less human interaction and, as a result, a more competitive financial offering.

Many companies and industries are in a quandary. Why do we still have our own sales team and an agents network if we can just blast this stuff online? So hybrids emerge, and uncertainties in the tenure of the ecosystem relationships appear as the pivot takes place.

Hotels hate paying exorbitant commissions (of up to 35% in some cases) to online travel agent sites such as booking.com. But booking.com delivers the attractive traffic levels and the eyeballs of travellers actively looking to make a booking so it's a difficult drug for hotels to withdraw from.

PayPal

PayPal has always been a 'payments' company, but it has gone through many permutations in the delivery channel. Initially the idea was to allow people to 'beam' payments from their PDAs (such as the Palm Pilot), the drawback being we had to meet face-to-face to make a transaction. That was clunky. So plan A was abandoned for Plan B, C, D, all the way to plan J. After merging with a financial services company called X.com, PayPal became the preferred online payment system for eBay, which made it the household name we know it as. But eBay recently discontinued their contract as the exclusive preferred payment system, so it looks like PayPal will need to possibly pivot again to find another more effective channel.

Honda

Honda made an almost laughable entry into the American motorcycle market in the 50s with its Supercub motorcycle. It looked like a toy next to the favoured chariot, Harley Davidson. It was too small, was too uncool and uncomfortable along Route 66, and motorcycle dealers could pocket more from selling a Harley.

Three strikes and out? No. Honda executives noticed that their customers had a different idea in mind — off-road riding. With this insight, Honda pivoted to distribute its bikes through sporting goods retailers. This signalled a different positioning altogether, and the dirt biking phenomenon took off.

This gave Honda an inroad (pardon the excruciating pun) and gained trust as a reliable machine, and in a classic *Innovator's Dilemma* play, progressively introduced bigger and better bikes and stole market share from under the incumbent's nose.

Kickstarter

Perry Chen was organising a jazz concert, and wanted to bring in a headline act for his festival from overseas. Problem was they were good and therefore expensive. Too much for Perry to personally bankroll. "What if we could ask those who might enjoy Jazzfest to commit to buying tickets?" So he asked his potential audience to kick in some money and, if enough was raised, the show could go on. And that, ladies and gentlemen, is how Kickstarter was Kickstarted. He found a more effective way to get good jazz to his audiences, therefore a classic channel pivot.

Scott Leggo Gallery

Scott is a Sydney-based photographer, and capitalizes on his love of the outdoors by being a landscape photographer who sells his photos online and through his gallery. Then Covid Lockdown struck. Quick as a flash (get it?) he thought, if customers can't come to me, I'll get to them – in a different form. He turned some of his most popular photo works into jigsaw puzzles, because – in a sort of Retro Pivot – these had become popular again in isolation. So now you can order a 250, 500 or 1000 piece landscape jigsaw from the comfort of your couch.

Technology Pivot

In which a new or different technology is deployed in order to achieve the same solution or output. A Technology Pivot is most relevantly used where a more competitive price or a superior performance is gained. In many ways this type of pivot typifies what pivoting is, because the fundamental outcome is the same (meaning many underlying elements are already in place and remain unchanged) but we found a smarter way behind the scenes to 'make' it.

So the 'job to do' doesn't change, neither the customer nor her problem changed, and our (sales and distribution) channel/s didn't change. This might bring to mind the ATM. All that happened is that a hole in the wall dispensed your cash instead of a bank clerk with a pen behind his ear. Which may reduce errors, and may save the bank salaries in the longer term.

Netflix

The master of successful Technology Pivoting. But through all of it the result never changed – you get to enjoy a movie at home. Netflix started out as a mail-order DVD service (with a monthly flat-fee subscription model rather a pay-per-view fee). It pivoted to downloadable films, then to streaming, then -- as competitive streaming services started bidding for the same content -- started to develop its own quality content: *Orange is the New Black, Stranger Things, Tiger King*.

"The goal is to become HBO, before HBO can become us," explained CEO, Reed Hastings. In 2018 they received more Emmy nominations than HBO.

If it hadn't pivoted away from mail-order DVDs, Netflix would have no doubt collapsed like a *House of Cards*. One of my favourite anecdotes regarding Netflix is told against the CEO of Blockbuster video when interviewed by *Harvard Business Review* in 2012: "Netflix? Haha, those guys aren't even on our radar." By 2014 Blockbuster had filed for bankruptcy. Haha, love it!

Which leaves us with the salient lesson: a good idea is never a good idea for all-time.

Western Union

Western Union started out as a telegram service, sending 200 million telegrams across the globe at its peak in 1929. However, as first the telephone and later the internet effectively killed off that technology, Western Union pivoted to focus on a number of diverse activities, the most successful of which was money transfer. But it might want to dust off its Pivot ToolBox because, as you'll read, Transferwise have seen they've had it too good for too long in the cash transfer game, plus there's the looming threat of what Blockchain might do to its business model.

Haier Electronics

When China emerged from its hermitic hibernation, many of its technologies were rather old school. A particularly motivated innovator, Zhang Ruimen, came into the Qingdao Refrigerator Plant when it was on the brink of failure, and staff hadn't been paid, in 1984. He gathered the entire factory team in an outside courtyard, and lined up around 70 of their appliances. He then took a sledgehammer to each and every one (appliances, not the team), declaring it substandard crap in a shocking and gob-smacking demonstration. They teamed up with a German technology partner, thereby leapfrogging several tech generations, and renamed the company Haier. They also did a Zoom-out Pivot, going to a full range of household appliances including air-cons and cookers. In 2016, Zhang oversaw their buy-out of GE Appliances for $5.4 billion, as GE was going through something like a Zoom-in Pivot at the time and off-loading all sorts of business units it had developed and acquired.

Gore

Sometimes it helps to understand customer needs better if *you* are the customer. Dave Evans was an engineer at Gore by day, but a keen mountain bike rider each weekend. He noticed the gear-changing of his brakes was a bit clunky due to the wire cables getting caked with dirt and rusting from water. And if it was a problem he needed solved, maybe there were thousands of others who needed a solution too. So, he set about experimenting with coating wires with a protective polymer tubing. That did the trick, and his ride was smoother with less maintenance. Gore launched the Ride-On system to much fanfare and success.

Evans was also a guitarist – and he had a problem with guitar strings. They rusted and, after repeated use, the sound lost its sharpness and sounded muffled. What if? Yes, he experimented with coating guitar strings in polymer coating and that solved both problems. Gore's Elixir strings are now the best-selling on the market even though they are triple the average price.

Retro Pivot

In this fast-and-furious future-facing world, we rarely stop and take a look in the rear vision mirror. Of our own products, our own company, or our own industry. Often great ideas and great value lies in the rubble of the past. Because all too often the really great, breakthrough, category-busting ideas are way ahead of their time.

For example: the electric car. What year was it invented? Give yourself a pat on the back if you said "1837." Then it died out. And suddenly Tesla made it the shiny and sexy thing again.

And look at the hipster barber shops doing brisk business with their 1920s décor, foamy lather, and strop razors.

So what old ideas can you beg, borrow, steal to bring new life to your company or start-up? It's well worth having a trawl through the local patent office to see what magic inspirations from ye olde days might just be the darling of tomorrow.

Music companies are doing it with the release of vinyl albums, sales of which are currently neck-and-neck with CDs, and poised to surpass them for the first time since 1986. Everything old is new again.

Robe Dairy

Robe, population 998, is a small coastal country town in South Australia. And there you'll find David and Julie Hinchliffe milking their Jersey cows to make milk, cheese and yoghurt. Then came Covid-19 and suddenly business dropped right off. They were fighting to keep their business alive. Then they did a Retro Pivot. If people weren't visiting Robe Foodland or The Veg Shed anymore, they'd take a leaf from the past and play milkman (and woman). So now you'll see them dropping off bottles of fresh dairy produce on the front door steps of those who order. It's brought back nostalgia to their customers, and brought their tiny community closer in a time of otherwise isolation. Many are asking them to keep doing this forever, please.

Dumb Luck Pivot

Sometimes you just get lucky. Call it serendipity, call it 'where hard work meets preparation.' In this type of pivot you stumble blindly into your new possible direction ... but that's not to underplay the important role of keen observation skills.

IKEA

In 1956 Gillis Lundgren was the catalog manager for Ikea (then a 13-year-old mail order company selling furniture, stockings and pens), and needed to take a rather sturdy leaf-shaped table to a nearby photo studio. Problem was he couldn't fit it into his little car. "I thought: Why not take off the legs?" Further thought on this issue made him realise that flat-packing would save a fortune in shipping costs, thus fitting better with Ikea's avowed low-price ambitions. While he didn't invent flat-packing – a fellow Swede had patented a ready-to-assemble chair in 1949 – Ikea popularized it and it was their growth catalyst and point of difference ever since.

Suzuki

I ride a Suzuki 650 V-Strom motorcycle. But they didn't start out life making motorbikes – in fact, until 1935 founder and inventor Michio Suzuki was best known for his weaving loom machines that powered Japan's silk industry. In looking to diversify as the market slowed, he leveraged his engineering strengths and moved towards making cars, but the war intervened. Post-war he made clip-on engines for bicycles, then 50cc motorbikes, then 125cc motorbikes in the mid-50s. In 1961 he had a stroke of luck when East German racer Ernst Degner defected with secrets of combustion chamber engines, and brought them straight to Suzuki. The following year Suzuki won the 500cc world championship!

Japan Railways East

In the 1980s Japan Railways East – one of the largest carriers of people in the world – was constructing a new high-speed railway line north of Tokyo. This involved creating a tunnel by drilling through the huge Mount Tanigawa. But water seepage hampered the engineers' progress. And one man's problem is another person's pivot. The workers loved the cool, clear refreshing waters, which was run-off from the ice caps above.

A maintenance worker made a radical suggestion: Why not bottle the water and sell it? So JR East entered the beverage business with a premium bottled mineral water, Oshimizu. Furthermore the company exploited its retail coverage by placing vending machines on over 1000 station platforms. The product line was extended to fruit juices and iced tea. Within 10 years sales of Oshimizu drinks were raking in over $50 million a year.

Slack

Today's beloved collaborative instant messaging and project management platform rose from the embers of a failed video game called Glitch. Someone on the game development team developed a style of communication which was a customised version of internet relay chat (something like an mIRC or ICQ to those who care about these things). Slack's founder, Stewart Butterfield, jokingly says that his team's super-effective instant communication platform sped up the demise of Glitch. Slack now has almost the same amount of users as Microsoft Teams.

Random Crazy Shit (RCS) Pivot

Ok, I said not to panic, because there's always a pivot to suit your need. But, what if you've come all the way down the list to here, and you're still fresh out of ideas? Our final opportunity is the RCS Pivot – do what the hell you have to in order to pay your bills and make money.

You could also call this a *Divot* – a desperate pivot you need to make because you're stuck in a deep hole!

No-one from an Ivy League Business School is going to hound you years from now and blame you for not performing a classic pivot. In fact they might just applaud your sheer unhinged brilliance. Like with Fusajira Yamauchi. Who? Read on ...

Nintendo

Yamauchi opened a 'flower card' shop in Kyoto back in 1889, just as the government was banning normal playing cards in order to kerb gambling. His shop was called '*Nintendo Koppai*'. Of course his cards – being the only ones available – proved highly popular and he built a great little business, eventually opening a second shop in Osaka. His son-in-law succeeded him in the business and the business continued to be a winning hand, then his grandson and then great-grandson took over – with innovations such as plastic coated cards and Disney character cards – until the time of the Tokyo Olympics in 1964 when the market became saturated.

The great-grandson performed an unusual People Pivot by firing anyone related to the family.

Then came the Zoom-out Pivot period where a wide variety of

other products were tried, none successfully. Then came President Hiroshi Yamauchi's desperate Random Crazy Shit Pivot period where nothing that had gone before was leveraged (and therefore you can argue it's not strictly a pivot).

Nintendo explored a number of different directions – including a taxi company, instant rice, and even by-the-hour 'love hotels'. Still no traction.

Then Nintendo forged a partnership with the hardware manufacturer, Sharp. Together, their engineers developed unique electronic toys like the Beam Gun. From there, the company made more rational expansions into home and arcade videogames, whose popularity was booming in the early 1970s.

They secured the rights to distribute the first video game console, the Magnavox Odyssey. Nintendo released its first console in 1977, and introduced (speaking of Random Crazy Shit) a hairy Italian plumber in dungarees called Super Mario to the world. Who would have thought there was pent-up consumer need for that? I don't think a hundred – or even a thousand – research surveys would've surfaced that one! Then came Nintendo Wii. Enough said.

And so, Nintendo, as we know it today, was off to the races. Hiroshi's net worth peaked at nearly $8 billion, the richest man in Japan. It took a few crazy zig zag pivots along the way, but you could say they got there in the end.

AGGREGATED TAKE-OUTS

So, what can we learn from all these examples of pivots and divots?

Focus on your future, not your legacy

When I work with Citibank, I tell them that what made them successful for the past 208 years is not what will make them successful for the next 208 years. No one owes you a living. Instead, focus on looming megatrends – and immediate needs in a crisis – and see how your business can morph towards and intersect with those.

Focus on outcomes, not on your process

Innovation though pivoting is about moving from What Is to What If? It's not about the current reality, it's about the future possibility. Possibility can be found by opening the strategic aperture of how you perceive your company and it's core competency (more on this in the Toolbox section). Don't stay married to a sunk-cost course if a better technology comes along, as Netflix showed us. Asking "What are we really trying to achieve here?" should distance you from your current process. If it makes it reassuring to know, The Rock and his business partner Dany Garcia have a rule: "We aren't attached to process. We're only attached to outcome." So there.

Focus on what's working well

Focus on the wins and strengths, and try to expand on them. Like Toys 'R Us and Instagram did. The other stuff is just deep-keel baggage that's holding you back. We need to focus just as much on what we *won't* and *don't* do, and destroy product lines, processes and mindsets that are not profitable nor performing to peak. This frees up resources to devote towards your creative pivot.

Cut your losses and run

Be passionate by all means. But do not get so gooey-eyed and emotionally involved with your idea that you go all the way down on your sinking ship. I've showcased some of the world's best entrepreneurs here, and all had the good sense to bail out when the getting out was good, and set their sails on another course so they could live to, not only fight another day, but emerge victorious. Such as the story with Glitch and Slack.

Pivot towards the money

Your business needs to make a buck to survive. Follow the money! Daydreams and ideals are one thing, but they might prove to be a limiting factor in a winning business model. Focus on where you can generate the most revenue – within the bounds of your values and principles. Nearly every example quoted here is about firstly surviving, but then ultimately thriving, be it Levi's, Haier or Play-Doh.

Pivoting is not a one-time thing

It's a continual zig-zag, an ongoing transformational process, to find the perfect wind. As we saw with PayPal, it took 10 iterations (Plan J) to get them to where they are today. Nintendo – countless. So your mindset needs to be one of restless dissatisfaction with the status quo in good times, and sweatily working the winches and the tiller in times of crisis.

THE 'PIVOT POWER' TOOLBOX

So you now have 20 powerful pivot methods at your disposal. Hopefully those have already sparked a boatload of ideas and possibilities.

Plus here are more systematic ways of going about the creative pivoting process. These are some of the most powerful tools I deploy to identify possible pivots.

Strategic Aperture tools

Let's start with the example of Bic. For 70 years they answered the question 'What business are you in?' by saying 'We're in the pen business.' Then came the fateful day when one of their executives answered: 'We're in the plastic disposable things business.' Zap! The electricity shot through the boardroom. Part-fear, part-excitement. Soon they came out with a plastic disposable razor, and within a few short financial years that business overtook pens as their biggest seller. The disposable razor market is now worth around $3 billion globally.

Another way to blast open the strategic aperture is by asking yourself:

'What business are we really, really, *really* in?

If you zoom out more broadly and focus on laddering up to the emotional benefit and outcomes, you will quickly push past the here and now of your reality and hopefully get a clearer view from 35,000 feet.

The following format works simply yet amazingly effectively by filling in the blanks with bravery. Remember, you are trying to bust open the aperture of possibility, rip off your blinkers. Tip: Try to move as far from the rational physical product or service as you can and aim for an emotional benefit.

We're not in the [x] business we're in the [y] business.

So, adidas might fill it out something like this:

**We're not in the footwear business we're in
the peak performance business.
We're not in the sports business we're in
the inspiration business.
We're not in the athletics wear business
we're in the health and wellness business.**

You can then start to reframe your value hypothesis by brainstorming along the lines of:

**'How might we help people achieve peak performance?'
'How might we inspire people?
'How might we deliver health and wellness?'**

As you can immediately feel, the answers will drop you off a long way from your starting point of 'We make running shoes.' There are sooooo many ways to answer that question and solve that problem for your customer or consumer.

Value Proposition Venn Tool

Draw a Venn diagram of two interlinking circles. Label one circle 'What customers/ consumers want *now*' and the other 'What *we* can do *best*.'

Make those lists, being sure to keep in mind that the consumer wants are up-to-the-minute fresh insights, because things unfold so rapidly in a crisis situation you don't want to be hitting last week's wants and needs. Too late!

And be exhaustive (and honest) with your own resources and competencies so that there's a clear point of difference from competitors, and a greater chance of sparking insight and spotting the common ground.

Write those down in the sweet spot. Now go and make that pivot happen.

The Bowtie Brainswarming Method

Another similar technique of finding the common ground sweet-spot, The Bowtie Brainswarm method revolves around identifying what people want/need, the consumers' reality in terms of megatrends, goals, problems and challenges, and then broadening, reducing and deconstructing the component parts of that on one hand.

At its broadest essence, what does this customer need or want?

On the other hand, you'll be inventorising what it is *you* have in terms of skills, resources, competencies and edge. Then you'll deconstruct that into its broad component parts.

Finally, synthesize by playing a game of good old 'find the matching parts' common to both sides. That's not your guaranteed final answer but *possibly* where your pivot opportunity lies. This is where you need to run a quick value test and knock-up some quick MVP prototypes.

This exercise is equally applicable to B2B and B2C applications, and could even create a Business Architecture Pivot in the process. You must have an open mind and leave yourself wide open to unexpected possibility in the process.

Let's use the example of a brewery amid the Covid Crisis ...

The illustration below uses the mass-market consumer as the target but of course you can substitute any potential consumer or customer buyer target.

You can see that there are quite a few broad match-ups to explore. But some are more low-hanging than others.

My gut feel is that we can do a Customer Segment Pivot to open up whole new markets (possibly they never did B2C before, having only supplied to pubs and retailers), and we can do a Customer Need Pivot to get sanitizer into their hands, literally.

Disruptive Thinking Tool

One of my favourite provocation questions when I facilitate disruptive thinking sessions is this one:

> **'If we were legally prohibited from selling our current products to our current customers, how would we make money next year?'**

It often starts out with a lot of blank stares because people are so entrenched in the status quo that they can't see any other ways. But this is exactly the situation many businesses find themselves in during the Covid Crisis. Bars, cafes, restaurants, music venues, sports and entertainment franchises, circuses, hotels. Then the knock-on domino effect to most other industries. So how else can we make money?

And, as we have seen, people can be ever so resourceful with a Smith & Wesson .38 against their head. Allow the ideas to be fun and fanciful – illegal and immoral even – because we can always pull them back into line later.

Brainstorming this question is really good preparation for the next crisis.

Value Testing Template

Is your idea a problem looking for a solution or a solution looking for a problem?

The best advice is to get your idea – however rough, raw or rudimentary – into your proposed customers' hands as quickly and cheaply as possible. They'll give you a good idea of whether it's solving their problem and represents actual value to them.

Gore, one of the world's most consistently innovative companies have a quick-fire checklist they apply to any candidate ideas. It's called 'Real/Win/Worth.'

Gore's Real/ Win/ Worth Checklist
REAL – does the invention solve a customer problem?
WIN – do we have the skills we need to make this a success?
WORTH – Can we make and sell this at a profit?

Let's take their example of the Elixir guitar strings we talked about before, and step through it:

REAL – It solves a distinct problem of dirty, muffled guitar strings.
WIN – We are skilled at coating wires, ie Ride-On bike cables.
WORTH – Guitarists would be willing to pay 3 x as much.

Tick, tick, tick. The idea is ready to move down the pipeline to the next gate stage.

And then test, test, test as you go along. As fast as you can, as cheaply as you can, to gain strategic certainty.

Short, Medium, Long Plans

We've already ascertained that doing is better than planning, especially in a crisis pivot or divot situation.

But you might want to sketch out 3-month, 6-month, and 12-month models to get an intuitive feel for how it could pan out. Longer than that – you're kidding yourself, nobody knows anything for sure. Anyway, we've got a crisis on our hands *now* to deal with.

I suggest the 12 Word Strategic Plan format, devised by Bernadette Jiwa, taking up no more than one page (12 point font size minimum, please!) ...

Fill in the blanks for your strategic plan/s:

DIRECTION: mission/ goal
RESULT: vision/ outcomes
HURDLES: potential obstacles
PLAN: action steps

READY. FIRE. AIM.

When I put these words up on a slide during a talk there's often a murmur in the crowd, and some embarrassed laughter: "Does he know he got the order wrong?"

Except I didn't.

Soldiers and gunners will often fire off some tracer rounds first (think of them as bullets in a high-viz vest), to get a sense of whether they are aiming too high, too low ... or in fact to establish whether there is actually something worth shooting at out there, or was it just a wild pig rustling in the bush?

So, you shoot first, *then* fine-tune your aim based on that. If you're waiting for the perfect headshot, chances are you'll be shot in the head first.

US Marines have a 'Fog of War' decision-making rule of thumb based on 70% certainty. Meaning, with bullets flying all around your head, if you're 70% sure the bad guys are in that hut, you take out that hut.

Better to execute an imperfect plan than to consider all angles and miss the opportunity.

Charles Lee, the chairman of Hong Kong's massive Lee Kum Kee group, is happy to execute on innovations at a 60% confidence level. They must be doing something right – his family has amassed a fortune worth over $8 billion.

So I'm going to add two more ways of working to guide your mindset at this crucial stage which are guaranteed to make you nervous:

Leap before you look.

Jump, then build a parachute on the way down.

Consider that LinkedIn co-founder Reid Hoffman says: "If you aren't embarrassed by your first product release, then you released it too late."

On Isokings' website new home page is a line of type: "Please excuse any errors, we literally put this together in the early hours of the morning!" Because they know speed trumps accuracy in this sort of crisis pivot or divot situation.

You might consider Pixar to be the paragon of perfection, but here's the surprising truth behind the scenes. "Early on, all our movies suck," co-founder Ed Catmull says. "Our job is to make them go from suck to not-suck. Reworking, reworking, reworking again until a flawed story finds its through line."

So not even the genii at Pixar nail it first time. In fact at a storytelling workshop in LA I was lucky enough to attend, director Pete Doctor (who wrote and/or directed *Monsters Inc, Up, Inside Out*, etc) shared that a typical 90-minute feature requires 12,000 drawings. But Pixar usually create 125,000 drawings to achieve that.

Meaning, they have a 90% "miss" rate as they pivot their way to another blockbuster hit.

Intel's Head of Innovation in China, Kapil Kane -- who's also worked behind the black curtain at Apple -- told me: "Innovation is a zig zag journey. You start with one thing in mind and end up with something completely different -- with many twists and turns, stops and goes along the way. You can never predict or plan the outcome of innovation. You just have to take a leap of faith and see where it takes you. Don't worry about the destination -- it's the journey that matters."

You're on that journey now. Because the harbour that was once safe for you, is not safe any longer. The sea is choppy, with a big storm forecast. You're fine-tuning the rigging. Trying to reposition yourself to find the perfect angle of wind for your sail. Harness the wind, and harvest it. Now hang on tight because this will be a hell of a ride.

Good luck and just remember: Don't panic – *pivot!*

—————

THE 'PIVOT POWER' PIVOT
BUSINESS CONSULTING

So you made it this far, and think that you possibly want or need to pivot your business. Good.

Whether you are a start-up, or in tech, retail, FMCG, CPG, banking, engineering, manufacturing, planning, or marketing, we can probably identify some really productive and profitable pivot opportunities for you:

Pivoting business strategy
Pivoting business model
Pivoting business plan
Pivoting brand strategy
Pivoting marketing strategy

Next step, please contact Stu Lloyd for a Discovery Call.

stu@hotheads-innovation.com
www.hotheads-innovation.com

ACKNOWLEDGEMENT

Thanks to my father, George, for teaching me to sail, shoot, and question the world.

Thanks to my brothers, Glendon and Roger, who share great memories of sailing and shooting with me, and remain the best mentors I have.

Bonus point awarded to Glendon for proofing my manuscript and pointing me towards some great pivot examples.

Thanks to my mother Jenny for sharing the joys of lockdown isolation with me when I suddenly found myself 'trapped' in Australia. Talk about pivoting!

ABOUT THE AUTHOR

Stu Lloyd

STU helps turbo-charge intra-preneurs' and entrepreneurs' creative thinking skills so that they can innovate better, stay relevant, and find the future faster.

CHIEF HOTHEAD at Hotheads Innovation, working with Fortune 500s such as Citbank, Adidas, Pfizer.

See: www.Hotheads-Innovation.com

CHIEF STORYTELLER at CatMatDog, where he unleashes the business storytelling power of executives so they can Captivate, Convince, and Convert better.

See: www.catmatdog.com

PRAISE FOR AUTHOR

The Perfect Storyteller!

- THE TELEGRAPH, UK

A Killer Book! This has really helped with both my classroom sessions and consulting projects. Good questions stimulate good answers. Well done!"

-JAMES REINNOLDT, ADJ. PROFESSOR, THE UNIVERSITY OF WASHINGTON.

More stimulating than a double shot of cold brew infused coffee. Full of energy, fresh bright ideas, and reminds you how something you think is already well explored has room to grow even more. Make mine a double!"

- DAVID FINCHER, FELLOW, AMD.

Stu boils ideas and insights down into digestible, actionable points that we can apply immediately to make us more effective, efficient and impactful in our work.

- WILL NEALY, SENIOR MANAGER, ADIDAS AMERICA.

BOOKS BY THIS AUTHOR

Swimming Up Waterfalls: A Playbook For Mavericks, Challengers And Intrapreneurs.

business creativity expert Stu Lloyd pushes, prods, probes, and provokes you to explore the outer-edges of reasonableness and possibility in business. Because that's where real the game-changing stuff lies.

This short, sharp and punchy playbook includes The Maverick Manifesto and a Cheat Sheet of 40 shape-shifting provocations to work on by yourself, or with your team.

Enjoy Stu's motivating riffs:
On the Maverick Mindset.
On Purpose and Culture.
On Strategic Thinking.
On Customer-centricity.
On Peak Performance.
On Creative Confidence & Fear of Failure.
On Creative Thinking & Problem Solving.

Killer Questions: How To Shape Better Questions To Shape Explosive Breakthroughs

Learn how to Rock the New Economy with Explosive Questioning, because creating better questions is the answer for challenging the status quo in today's uncertain business world.

-Find out the Killer Questions that kick-started empires like Air-BNB, Warby Parker, Starbucks, Gatorade, Air Asia, Pandora, Google, Amazon, Harry Potter, and Kickstarter.

-Learn how companies like P&G, Apple, Dyson, JetBlue, Disney, Dove, Mercedes F1, Pixar, and Gore use Killer Questions to develop blockbuster new products, experiences and marketing messages.

-How to identify and eradicate your cognitive blindspots.

-How to create a Curiosity Gap (and why that's so important).

-Why it's important to challenge the Status Quo and how to do it.

iNCLUDES THE KILLER QUESTIONS 9-STEP INNOVATION QUESTION FORMULA CANVAS

What Would Elon Do?: 100 Perception-Shifting Provocations For Managers, Marketers And Mavericks.

100 exciting ways to surface explosive insights, campaigns and strategies, instantly.

The 100 Provocations are divided between 9 chapters:
passion & purpose
strategy
challenging the status quo
product development
problem-solving & troubleshooting
sales & marketing
customer-centric
competitors
wtf? – where's the future?